COLIN DE GRANDHOMME

NEW ZEALAND CRICKETER

MR VIVEK KUMAR PANDEY

Made with ♥ on the Notion Press Platform
www.notionpress.com

Contents

Foreword

Short Biography Of Colin de Grandhomme & Life Style, Career etc. During Writing This Book No Character, No Religion & No Caste Are Harmed. It's Only For Study Purpose. We don't want to hurt anyone.

Preface

Author biography in English :

MY NAME IS VIVEK KUMAR PANDEY . I WAS BORN IN 30 SEP 2002,I AM FROM SURAT GUJARAT INDIA.MY DREAM WAS TO BE GOOD WRITERS ,MY FAMILY SUPPORTED ME TO SUCCESSFUL AND I CAN DO IT MY SELF.How do I write? That is a question, I believe, that can be honestly answered by me."CELEBRATING YOUNGEST WRITER AWARD WINNER IN GUJARAT 1ST RANK" MR PANDEY JI . I may think I did a good job writing something. The reader is the one who decides the quality of my writing. I do find writing to be natural to me and therefore find it to be a real challenge. My trick as a challenged writer is to do the best I can and know that I am happy with the final outcome. It may take a while to do my best and there may be quite a few problems I run into along the way.

I am not a greedy person those who are thinking about me and my self I never tried it anyone people suffering from sadness ,I trying to get promoted people suffering from happiness and joy in your Life Time. Now in current situation in India and also world people are unemployed and have no many but our indian governor help to people to get free food from ration card , i also take part in leadership team ,i am Motivational speaker , Film script writer. There was my two dream firstly writer and secondly actor & also my own film is upcoming soon i done almost completely completed script for my film .I AM GOING TO SAY WORD OF HEART TOUCH OUT PLEASE READ IT" , firstly i thanks my father he supports me in this field they always getting inspired me by own his words and behavior ,they always said that he was a biggest person in the world in future and also they purchase fruit and chocolate for me in anytime & anyway , firstly my father buy him then call me Vivek you want a chocolate i will say yes papa but how many tell me ,papa: you tell me how much i buy him i told 1 or 2 chocolate but my father purchase whole the boxes of chocolate and they get suprised me. MY FATHER WAS BORN IN " 20 SEPTEMBER" 1971 IN INDIA.

1) MY FATHER FAVORITE CLOTHES IS KURTA PAIJMA AND ALSO STYLES SHOE

2) FAVORITE SINGER IS KISHORE DA

3) FAVORITE STATE GUJARAT AND KOLKATA , HIS VILLAGE IN BIHAR

4) FAVORITE COLOR BLACK AND WHITE

THEY ALSO LOVE cricket like IPL and one day t-20 .they also like watching a News daily and heard the song daily ,they also interested in tik tok video but in current time tik tok is banned in india but also few videos are in you tube. In lockdown time my family and me very enjoy day daily. my father play daily ludo with his sister and son, daughter.they always loved tea and coffee anytime call me . I make it tea for my father but some reason after the April to june they are suffering from fever and cough , weakness on 6 June 2020 my father death. they not told me say bye bye his life. After death of 6 June on 10 june my mom and dad anniversary.but my father is Best in the world they can do anything for me please take care of father and respect it of your parents.

ONE

Colin de Grandhomme

- **Colin de Grandhomme**

1. Short Biography Of Colin de Grandhomme& Life Style, Career etc. During Writing This Book No Character, No Religion & No Caste Are Harmed. It's Only For Study Purpose. We don't want to hurt anyone.

- **Domestic and T20 career**

Born in Harare, de Grandhomme, who attended St. George's College, Harare, began his career by playing for Manicaland in Zimbabwe, and was part of the Zimbabwe team at the 2004 Under-19 Cricket World Cup in Bangladesh. He played for Auckland in New Zealand domestic cricket from 2006 until 2018. In 2017, he played in England for Warwickshire County Cricket Club after having played for Kolkata Knight Riders in the 2017 Indian Premier League.

In May 2018, he signed for Northern Districts ahead of the 2018–19 New Zealand domestic season. He played for Royal Challengers Bangalore in the 2018 and 2019 IPL seasons. In May 2021, he was signed by Hampshire for the T20 Blast. In 2021, he was drafted by Southern Brave for the inaugural season of The Hundred.

- **Colin De Grandhomme International career**

After representing Zimbabwe in the U19 World Cup, de Grandhomme moved to New Zealand, making his international debut on 11 February 2012 in a Twenty20 International against Zimbabwe. His One Day International (ODI) debut came against South Africa on 3 March 2012. In November 2016, de Grandhomme was named in New Zealand's Test squad for the side against the touring Pakistanis and debuted in the first Test match on 17 November. He scored a half-century and took a five-wicket haul on debut, winning the player of the match award.On 2 December 2017, against the touring West Indies, de Grandhomme scored his first Test century. The 71-ball century was the second-fastest century in Tests by a New Zealand batsman. He left the tour ahead of the ODI matches against the West Indies after the death of his father in Zimbabwe.

In May 2018, de Grandhomme was one of twenty players to be awarded a new contract for the 2018–19 season by New Zealand Cricket. In April 2019, he was named in New Zealand's squad for the 2019 Cricket World Cup. He announced his retirement from international cricket on 31st August 2022.

TWO

NEW ZEALAND NATIONAL CRICKET TEAM

- **New Zealand national cricket team**

The New Zealand national cricket team represents New Zealand in men's international cricket. Named the Black Caps, they played their first Test in 1930 against England in Christchurch, becoming the fifth country to play Test cricket. From 1930 New Zealand had to wait until 1956, more than 26 years, for its first Test victory, against the West Indies at Eden Park in Auckland. They played their first ODI in the 1972–73 season against Pakistan in Christchurch.

The current captain in all formats of the game is Kane Williamson, who replaced Brendon McCullum after the latter's retirement in December 2015. The national team is organised by New Zealand Cricket.

The New Zealand cricket team became known as the Blackcaps in January 1998, after its sponsor at the time, Clear Communications, held a competition to choose a name for the team. This is one of many national team nicknames related to the All Blacks.

- As of 19th November 2021, New Zealand have played 1383 international matches, winning 539, losing 618, tying 15 and drawing 167 matches while 44 matches ended as no result. The team is ranked 1st in Tests, 1st in ODIs and 3rd in T20Is by the ICC. New Zealand have reached two World Cup finals, in 2015 and 2019. They defeated South Africa in the semi final of the 2015 World Cup, which was their first win in the a world cup semi final, but they ultimately lost to Trans-Tasman rivals Australia. In the next World Cup in 2019, New Zealand again reached the final which they lost to the hosts England on boundary count after the match and the subsequent Super Over both ended as ties.

The 2000 ICC KnockOut Trophy win (now referred to as ICC Champions Trophy) stands as one of two ICC tournaments won by the team in their cricketing history. New Zealand also won the inaugural ICC World Test Championship tournament in 2021, beating India by 8 wickets.

- **Beginnings of cricket in New Zealand**

The reverend Henry Williams provided history with the first report of a game of cricket in New Zealand, when he wrote in his diary in December 1832 about boys in and around Paihia on Horotutu Beach playing cricket. In 1835,

Charles Darwin and HMS Beagle called into the Bay of Islands on its epic circumnavigation of the Earth and Darwin witnessed a game of cricket played by freed Māori slaves and the son of a missionary at Waimate North. Darwin in The Voyage of the Beagle wrote.

several young men redeemed by the missionaires from slavery were employed on the farm. In the evening I saw a party of them at cricket.

The first recorded game of cricket in New Zealand took place in Wellington in December 1842. The Wellington Spectator reports a game on 28 December 1842 played by a "Red" team and a "Blue" team from the Wellington Club. The first fully recorded match was reported by the Examiner in Nelson between the Surveyors and Nelson in March 1844.

The first team to tour New Zealand was Parr's all England XI in 1863–64. Between 1864 and 1914, 22 foreign teams toured New Zealand. England sent 6 teams, Australia 15 and one from Fiji.

- **First national team**

On 15–17 February 1894 the first team representing New Zealand played New South Wales at Lancaster Park in Christchurch. New South Wales won by 160 runs. New South Wales returned again in 1895–96 and New Zealand won the solitary game by 142 runs, its first victory. The New Zealand Cricket Council was formed towards the end of 1894.

New Zealand played its first two internationals (not Tests) in 1904–05 against a star-studded Australia team containing such players as Victor Trumper, Warwick Armstrong and Clem Hill. Rain saved New Zealand from a thrashing in the first match, but not the second, which

New Zealand lost by an innings and 358 runs – currently the second largest defeat in New Zealand first-class history.

- **Inter-war period**

In 1927 NZ toured England. They played 26 first-class matches, mostly against county sides. They won seven matches, including those against Worcestershire, Glamorgan, Somerset and Derbyshire. On the strength of the performances of this tour New Zealand was granted Test status.

In 1929/30 the M.C.C toured NZ and played 4 Tests all of 3 days in duration. New Zealand lost its first Test match but drew the next 3. In the second Test Stewie Dempster and Jackie Mills put on 276 for the first wicket. This is still the highest partnership for New Zealand against England. New Zealand first played South Africa in 1931–32 in a three match series but were unable to secure Test matches against any teams other than England before World War II ended all Test cricket for 7 years. A Test tour by Australia, planned for February and March 1940, was cancelled after the outbreak of the war.

- **After World War II**

New Zealand's first Test after the war was against Australia in 1945/46. This game was not considered a "Test" at the time but it was granted Test status retrospectively by the International Cricket Council in March 1948. The New Zealand players who appeared in this match probably did not appreciate this move by the ICC as New Zealand were dismissed for 42 and 54. The New Zealand Cricket Council's unwillingness to pay Australian players a decent allowance to tour New Zealand ensured that this was the only Test Australia played against New Zealand between 1929 and 1972.

In 1949 New Zealand sent one of its best ever sides to England. It contained Bert Sutcliffe, Martin Donnelly, John R. Reid and Jack Cowie. However, 3-day Test matches ensured that all 4 Tests were drawn. Many have regarded the 1949 tour of England among New Zealand's best ever touring performances. All four tests were high-scoring despite being draws and Martin Donnelly's 206 at Lord's hailed as one of the finest innings ever seen there. Despite being winless, New Zealand did not lose a test either. Prior to this, only the legendary 1948 Australian team, led by the great Don Bradman, had achieved this.

New Zealand played its first matches against the West Indies in 1951–52, and Pakistan and India in 1955/56.

In 1954/55 New Zealand recorded the lowest ever innings total, 26 against England. The following season New Zealand achieved its first Test victory. The first 3 Tests of a 4 Test series were won easily by the West Indies but New Zealand won the fourth to notch up its first Test victory. It had taken them 45 matches and 26 years to attain.

- **New Zealand vs West Indies**

255 all out (166.5 overs)
John R. Reid 84
Tom Dewdney 5/21 (19.5 overs)
145 all out (78.3 overs)
Hammond Furlonge 64
Harry Cave 4/22 (27.3 overs)
157 all out (80 overs)
Sammy Guillen 41

Denis Atkinson 7/53 (40 overs)

77 all out (45.1 overs)

Everton Weekes 31

Harry Cave 4/21 (13.1 overs)

New Zealand won by 190 runs

Eden Park, Auckland

Umpires: Clyde Harris (NZL) and Terry Pearce (NZL)

- **New Zealand won the toss and chose to bat**

In the next 20 years New Zealand won only seven more Tests. For most of this period New Zealand lacked a class bowler to lead their attack although they had two excellent batsmen in Bert Sutcliffe and Glenn Turner and a great all-rounder in John R. Reid.

Reid captained New Zealand on a tour to South Africa in 1961–62 where the five test series was drawn 2–2. The victories in the third and fifth tests were the first overseas victories New Zealand achieved. Reid scored 1,915 runs in the tour, setting a record for the most runs scored by a touring batsman of South Africa as a result.

New Zealand won their first test series in their three match 1969/70 tour of Pakistan 1–0.This was the first ever series win by New Zealand after almost 40 years and 30 consecutive winless series.

- **1970 to 2000**

Scoreboard - Basin ReserveFebruary 1978. NZ's first win over England

In 1973 Richard Hadlee debuted and the rate at which New Zealand won Tests picked up dramatically. Hadlee was one of the best pace bowlers of his generation, playing 86

Tests for New Zealand, before he retired in 1990. Of the 86 Tests that Hadlee played in New Zealand won 22 and lost 28. In 1977/78 New Zealand won its first Test against England, at the 48th attempt. Hadlee took 10 wickets in the match.

During the 1980s New Zealand also had the services of one of its best ever batsman, Martin Crowe and a number of good players such as John Wright, Bruce Edgar, John F. Reid, Andrew Jones, Geoff Howarth, Jeremy Coney, Ian Smith, John Bracewell, Lance Cairns, Stephen Boock, and Ewen Chatfield, who were capable of playing the occasional match winning performance and consistently making a valuable contribution to a Test match.

The best example of New Zealand's two star players (R. Hadlee and M. Crowe) putting in match winning performances and other players making good contributions is New Zealand versus Australia, 1985 at Brisbane. In Australia's first innings Hadlee took 9–52. In New Zealand's only turn at bat, M Crowe scored 188 and John F. Reid 108. Edgar, Wright, Coney, Jeff Crowe, V. Brown, and Hadlee scored between 17 and 54*. In Australia's second innings, Hadlee took 6–71 and Chatfield 3–75. New Zealand won by an innings and 41 runs.

8–12 November 1985

Scorecard

- **Australia vs New Zealand**

179 (76.4 overs)

Kepler Wessels 70 (186)

Richard Hadlee 9/52 (23.4 overs)

553/7d (161 overs)

Martin Crowe 188 (328)

Greg Matthews 3/110 (31 overs)

333 (116.5 overs
Allan Border 152* (301)
Richard Hadlee 6/71 (28.5 overs)
New Zealand won by an innings and 41 runs
The Gabba, Brisbane
Umpires: Tony Crafter (Aus) and Dick French (Aus)
Player of the match: Richard Hadlee (NZ)

- **New Zealand won the toss and elected to field.**

One-day cricket also gave New Zealand a chance to compete more regularly than Test cricket with the better sides in world cricket. In one-day cricket a batsman does not need to score centuries to win games for his side and bowlers do not need to bowl the opposition out. One-day games can be won by one batsman getting a 50, a few others getting 30s, bowlers bowling economically and everyone fielding well. These were requirements New Zealand players could consistently meet and thus developed a good one-day record against all sides.

Perhaps New Zealand's most infamous one-day match was the "under arm" match against Australia at the MCG in 1981. Requiring six runs to tie the match off the final ball, Australian captain Greg Chappell instructed his brother Trevor to "bowl" the ball underarm along the wicket to prevent New Zealand batsman Brian McKechnie from hitting a six. The Australian umpires ruled the move as legal even though to this day many believe it was one of the most unsporting decisions made in cricket.

When New Zealand next played in the tri-series in Australia in 1983, Lance Cairns became a cult hero for his one-day batting. In one match against Australia, he hit six sixes at the MCG, one of the world's largest grounds. Few fans remember that New Zealand lost this game by 149 runs. However, Lance's greatest contribution to New Zealand cricket was his son Chris Cairns.

Chris Cairns made his debut one year before Hadlee retired in 1990. Cairns, one of New Zealand's best all-rounders, led the 1990s bowling attack with Danny Morrison. Stephen Fleming, New Zealand's most prolific scorer, led the batting and the team into the 21st century. Nathan Astle and Craig McMillan also scored plenty of runs for New Zealand, but both retired earlier than expected.

Daniel Vettori made his debut as an 18-year-old in 1997, and when he took over from Fleming as captain in 2007 he was regarded as the best spinning all-rounder in world cricket. On 26 August 2009, Daniel Vettori became the eighth player and second left-arm bowler (after Chaminda Vaas) in history to take 300 wickets and score 3000 test runs, joining the illustrious club. Vettori decided to take an indefinite break from international short form cricket in 2011 but continued to represent New Zealand in Test cricket and returned for the 2015 Cricket World Cup.

On 4 April 1996, New Zealand achieved a unique world record, where the whole team was adjudged Man of the Match for team performance against 4 run victory over the West Indies. This is recorded as the only time where whole team achieved such an award.

- **The Black Caps logo.**

New Zealand started the new millennium by winning the 2000 ICC KnockOut Trophy in Kenya to claim their first ICC tournament. They started with a 64-run win over Zimbabwe then proceeded to beat Pakistan by 4 wickets in the semi-final. In the final against India, Chris Cairns scored an unbeaten 102 in New Zealand's run chase helping them win the tournament.

- **New Zealand won the 2000 ICC Knockout Trophy.**

Shane Bond played 17 Tests for NZ between 2001 and 2007 but missed far more through injury. When fit, he added a dimension to the NZ bowling attack that had been missing since Hadlee retired.

- **The New Zealand team celebrating a dismissal in 2009**

The rise of the financial power of the BCCI had an immense effect on NZ cricket and its players. The BCCI managed to convince other boards not to pick players who had joined the rival Twenty-20 Indian Cricket League. NZ Cricket lost the services of Shane Bond, Lou Vincent, Andre Adams, Hamish Marshall and Daryl Tuffey. The money to be made from Twenty-20 cricket in India may have also induced players, such as Craig McMillan and Scott Styris (from Test cricket) to retire earlier than they would have otherwise. After the demise of the Indian Cricket League Bond and Tuffey again played for New Zealand.

Vettori stood down as Test captain in 2011 leading to star batsman Ross Taylor to take his place. Taylor led New Zealand for a year which included a thrilling win in a low scoring Test match against Australia in Hobart, their first win over Australia since 1993. In 2012/13 Brendon McCullum became captain and new players such as Kane Williamson, Corey Anderson, Doug Bracewell, Trent Boult and Jimmy Neesham emerged as world-class performers. McCullum captained New Zealand to series wins against the West Indies and India in 2013/14 and both Pakistan and Sri Lanka in 2014/15 increasing New Zealand's rankings in both Test and ODI formats. In the series against India McCullum scored 302 at Wellington to become New Zealand's first Test triple centurion.

1. In early 2015 New Zealand made the final of the Cricket World Cup, going through the tournament undefeated until the final, where they lost to Australia by seven wickets.
2. In 2015 the New Zealand national cricket team played under the name of Aotearoa for their first match against Zimbabwe to celebrate te Wiki o te Reo Māori (Māori Language Week).
3. In mid-2015 New Zealand toured England, performing well, drawing the Test series 1–1, and losing the One Day series, 2–3.
4. From October to November 2015, and in February 2016, New Zealand played Australia in two Test Series, in three and two games a piece
5. With a changing of an era in the Australian team, New Zealand was rated as a chance of winning especially in New Zealand. New Zealand lost both series by 2-0

THREE

HISTORY OF CRICKET

- **History of cricket**

The sport of cricket has a known history beginning in the late 16th century. Having originated in south-east England, it became an established sport in the country in the 18th century and developed globally in the 19th and 20th centuries. International matches have been played since the 19th-century and formal Test cricket matches are considered to date from 1877. Cricket is the world's second most popular spectator sport after association football (soccer).

Internationally, cricket is governed by the International Cricket Council (ICC) which has over one hundred countries and territories in membership although only twelve currently play Test cricket.

- **Origin**

Cricket was probably created during Saxon or Norman times by children living in the Weald, an area of dense woodlands and clearings in south-east England that lies across Kent and Sussex. The first definite written reference is from the end of the 16th-century.

There have been several speculations about the game's origins, including some that it was created in France or Flanders. The earliest of these speculative references is from 1300 and concerns the future King Edward II playing at "creag and other games" in both Westminster and Newenden. It has been suggested that "creag" was an Old English word for cricket, but expert opinion is that it was an early spelling of "craic", meaning "fun and games in general".

It is generally believed that cricket survived as a children's game for many generations before it was increasingly taken up by adults around the beginning of the 17th century. Possibly cricket was derived from bowls, assuming bowls is the older sport, by the intervention of a batsman trying to stop the ball from reaching its target by hitting it away. Playing on sheep-grazed land or in clearings, the original implements may have been a matted lump of sheep's wool (or even a stone or a small lump of wood) as the ball; a stick or a crook or another farm tool as the bat; and a stool or a tree stump or a gate (e.g., a wicket gate) as the wicket.

- **First definite reference**

John Derrick was a pupil at the Royal Grammar School, then the Free School, in Guildford when he and his friends played creckett circa 1550.

In 1597 (Old Style – 1598 New Style) a court case in England concerning an ownership dispute over a plot of common land in Guildford, Surrey, mentions the game of creckett. A 59-year-old coroner, John Derrick, testified that he and his school friends had played creckett on the site fifty years earlier when they attended the Free School. Derrick's account proves beyond reasonable doubt that the game was being played in Surrey circa 1550, and is the earliest universally accepted reference to the game.

The first reference to cricket being played as an adult sport was in 1611, when two men in Sussex were prosecuted for playing cricket on Sunday instead of going to church. In the same year, a dictionary defined cricket as a boys‘ game, and this suggests that adult participation was a recent development.

- **Derivation of the name of "cricket"**

A number of words are thought to be possible sources for the term "cricket". In the earliest definite reference, it was spelled creckett. The name may have been derived from the Middle Dutch krick(-e), meaning a stick; or the Old English cricc or cryce meaning a crutch or staff, or the French word criquet meaning a wooden post. The Middle Dutch word krickstoel means a long low stool used for kneeling in church; this resembled the long low wicket with two stumps used in early cricket. According to Heiner Gillmeister, a European language expert of the University of Bonn, "cricket" derives from the Middle Dutch phrase for hockey, met de (krik ket)sen (i.e., "with the stick chase").

It is more likely that the terminology of cricket was based on words in use in south-east England at the time and, given trade connections with the County of Flanders, especially in the 15th century when it belonged to the Duchy of Burgundy, many Middle Dutch words found their way into southern English dialects.

- **The Commonwealth**

After the Civil War ended in 1648, the new Puritan government clamped down on "unlawful assemblies", in particular the more raucous sports such as football. Their laws also demanded a stricter observance of the Sabbath than there had been previously. As the Sabbath was the only free time available to the lower classes, cricket's popularity may have waned during the Commonwealth. However, it did flourish in public fee-paying schools such as Winchester and St Paul's. There is no actual evidence that Oliver Cromwell's regime banned cricket specifically and there are references to it during the interregnum that suggest it was acceptable to the authorities provided that it did not cause any "breach of the Sabbath". It is believed that the nobility in general adopted cricket at this time through involvement in village games.

- **Gambling and press coverage**

Cricket thrived after the Restoration in 1660 and is believed to have first attracted gamblers making large bets at this time. It is possible, as believed by some historians, that top-class matches began. In 1664, the "Cavalier" Parliament passed the Gaming Act 1664 which limited stakes to £100, although that was still a fortune at the time, equivalent to about £16,000 in present-day terms. Cricket had become a significant gambling sport by the end of the 17th century, as evidenced in 1697 by a newspaper report of a "great match" played in Sussex which was 11-a-side and played for high stakes of 50 guineas a side.

With freedom of the press having been granted in 1696, cricket for the first time could be reported in the newspapers. But it was a long time before the newspaper industry adapted sufficiently to provide frequent, let alone comprehensive, coverage of the game. During the first half of the 18th century, press reports tended to focus on the betting rather than on the play.

- **18th-century cricket**

Gambling introduced the first patrons because some of the gamblers decided to strengthen their bets by forming their own teams and it is believed the first "county teams" were formed in the aftermath of the Restoration in 1660, especially as members of the nobility were employing "local experts" from village cricket as the earliest professionals. The first known game in which the teams use county names is in 1709 but there can be little doubt that these sort of fixtures were being arranged long before that. The match in 1697 was probably Sussex versus another county.

The most notable of the early patrons were a group of aristocrats and businessmen who were active from about 1725, which is the time that press coverage became more regular, perhaps as a result of the patrons' influence. These men included the 2nd Duke of Richmond, Sir William Gage, Alan Brodrick and Edwin Stead. For the first time, the press mentions individual players like Thomas Waymark.

- **Cricket expands beyond England**

Cricket was introduced to North America via the English colonies in the 17th century, probably before it had even reached the north of England. In the 18th century it arrived in other parts of the globe. It was introduced to the West Indies by colonists and to India by East India Company mariners in the first half of the century. It arrived in Australia almost as soon as colonisation began in 1788. New Zealand and South Africa followed in the early years of the 19th century.

Cricket never caught on in Canada, despite efforts by the upper class to promote the game as a way of identifying with the "mother country". Canada, unlike Australia and the West Indies, witnessed a continual decline in the popularity of the game during 1860 to 1960. Linked in the public consciousness to an upper-class sport, the game never became popular with the general public. In the summer season it had to compete with baseball. During the First World War, Canadian units stationed in France played baseball instead of cricket.

- **Development Laws of Cricket**

It's not clear when the basic rules of cricket such as bat and ball, the wicket, pitch dimensions, overs, how out, etc. were originally formulated. In 1728, the Duke of Richmond and Alan Brodick drew up Articles of Agreement to determine the code of practice in a particular game and this became a common feature, especially around payment of stake money and distributing the winnings given the importance of gambling.

In 1744, the Laws of Cricket were codified for the first time and then amended in 1774, when innovations such as lbw, middle stump and maximum bat width were added.

These laws stated that "the principals shall choose from amongst the gentlemen present two umpires who shall absolutely decide all disputes". The codes were drawn up by the so-called "Star and Garter Club" whose members ultimately founded the Marylebone Cricket Club at Lord's in 1787. The MCC immediately became the custodian of the Laws and has made periodic revisions and recodifications subsequently.

- **Continued growth in England**

The game continued to spread throughout England, and, in 1751, Yorkshire is first mentioned as a venue. The original form of bowling (i.e., rolling the ball along the ground as in bowls) was superseded sometime after 1760 when bowlers began to pitch the ball and study variations in line, length and pace. Scorecards began to be kept on a regular basis from 1772; since then, an increasingly clear picture has emerged of the sport's development.

- **An artwork depicting the history of the cricket bat**

The first famous clubs were London and Dartford in the early 18th century. London played its matches on the Artillery Ground, which still exists. Others followed, particularly Slindon in Sussex, which was backed by the Duke of Richmond and featured the star player Richard Newland. There were other prominent clubs at Maidenhead, Hornchurch, Maidstone, Sevenoaks, Bromley, Addington, Hadlow and Chertsey.

But far and away the most famous of the early clubs was Hambledon in Hampshire. It started as a parish organisation that first achieved prominence in 1756. The club itself was founded in the 1760s and was well patronised to the extent that it was the focal point of the game for about thirty years until the formation of MCC and the opening of Lord's Cricket Ground in 1787. Hambledon produced several outstanding players including the master batsman John Small and the first great fast bowler Thomas Brett. Their most notable opponent was the Chertsey and Surrey bowler Edward "Lumpy" Stevens, who is believed to have been the main proponent of the flighted delivery.

It was in answer to the flighted, or pitched, delivery that the straight bat was introduced. The old "hockey stick"–style of bat was only really effective against the ball being trundled or skimmed along the ground. First-class cricket began, retrospectively, in 1772.A Game of Cricket at The Royal Academy Club in Marylebone Fields, now Regent's Park, depiction by unknown artist, c. 1790–1799

- **History of cricket (1772–1815) and History of English cricket (1816–1863)**

The game also underwent a fundamental change of organisation with the formation for the first time of county clubs. All the modern county clubs, starting with Sussex in 1839, were founded during the 19th century. No sooner had the first county clubs established themselves than they faced what amounted to "player action" as William Clarke created the travelling All-England Eleven in 1846. Though a commercial venture, this team did much to popularise the game in districts which had never previously been visited by high-class cricketers. Other similar teams were created and this vogue lasted for about thirty years. But the counties and MCC prevailed.

- **A cricket match at Darnall, Sheffield in the 1820s.**

The growth of cricket in the mid and late 19th century was assisted by the development of the railway network. For the first time, teams from a long distance apart could play one other without a prohibitively time-consuming journey. Spectators could travel longer distances to matches, increasing the size of crowds. Army units around the Empire had time on their hands, and encouraged the locals so they could have some entertaining competition. Most of the Empire embraced cricket, with the exception of Canada.

In 1864, another bowling revolution resulted in the legalisation of overarm and in the same year. W. G. Grace began his long and influential career at this time, his feats doing much to increase cricket's popularity. He introduced technical innovations which revolutionised the game, particularly in batting.

- **International cricket begins**

The first ever international cricket game was between the US and Canada in 1844. The match was played at the grounds of the St George's Cricket Club in New York.

- **The English team 1859 on their way to the US**

In 1859, a team of leading English professionals set off to North America on the first-ever overseas tour and, in 1862, the first English team toured Australia. Between May and October 1868, a team of Aboriginal Australians toured England in what was the first Australian cricket team to travel overseas.

- **The first Australian touring team (1878) pictured at Niagara Falls**

In 1877, an England touring team in Australia played two matches against full Australian XIs that are now regarded as the inaugural Test matches. The following year, the Australians toured England for the first time and the success of this tour ensured a popular demand for similar ventures in future. No Tests were played in 1878 but more soon followed and, at The Oval in 1882, the Australian victory in a tense finish gave rise to The Ashes.South Africa became the third Test nation in 1889.

- **National championships**

A significant development in domestic cricket occurred in 1890 when the official County Championship was constituted in England. Soon afterwards, in May 1894, the sport's first-class standard was officially defined. This organisational initiative has been repeated in other countries. Australia established the Sheffield Shield in 1892–93. Other national competitions to be established were the Currie Cup in South Africa, the Plunket Shield in New Zealand and the Ranji Trophy in India. The ICC re-defined first-class status in 1947 as a global concept.

The period from 1890 to the outbreak of the First World War has become one of nostalgia, ostensibly because the teams played cricket according to "the spirit of the game", but more realistically because it was a peacetime period that was shattered by the First World War. The era has been called The Golden Age of cricket and it featured numerous great names such as Grace, Wilfred Rhodes, C. B. Fry, Ranjitsinhji and Victor Trumper.

- **Balls per over**

During most of the 19th-century standard overs were made up of four deliveries. In 1889 five-ball overs were introduced in first-class cricket, with a move to generally use six-ball overs in 1900.

In the 20th-century, eight-ball overs were used at times in a number of countries, primarily Australia, where eight-balls were the standard over length between 1918/19 and 1978/79, South Africa and New Zealand. Since the 1979/80 Australian and New Zealand seasons, six balls per over have been used worldwide, and the most recent version of the Laws only permits six-ball overs.

- **Growth of international cricket**

Sid Barnes traps Lala Amarnath lbw in the first official Test between Australia and India at the MCG in 1948

The Imperial Cricket Conference was founded in 1909 with England, Australia and South Africa as the founder members. This aimed to regulate international cricket between the three sides, considered the only three of equal status at the time. West Indies were admitted as members in 1928, allowing them to play Test cricket against the other sides. New Zealand and India both became Test playing nations before World War II and Pakistan joined soon afterwards in 1952.

At the initial suggestion of Pakistan, the ICC was expanded to include non-Test playing countries from 1965, with Associate members being admitted. At the same time the organisation changed its name to the International Cricket Conference. The first limited-overs World Cups were played during the 1970s and Sri Lanka became the first

Associate member to be raised to Test playing status in 1982.

The international game continued to grow with the introduction of Affiliate Member status in 1984, a level of membership designed for sides with less history of playing cricket. In 1989 the ICC renamed itself the International Cricket Council. Zimbabwe became Full Members in 1992 and Bangladesh in 2000 before Afghanistan and Ireland were both admitted as Test sides in 2018, bringing the number of full members of the ICC to 12.

- **International cricket in South Africa from 1971 to 1981**

The greatest crisis to hit international cricket was brought about by apartheid, the South African policy of racial segregation. The situation began to crystallise after 1961 when South Africa left the Commonwealth of Nations and so, under the rules of the day, its cricket board had to leave the International Cricket Conference (ICC). Cricket's opposition to apartheid intensified in 1968 with the cancellation of England's tour to South Africa by the South African authorities, due to the inclusion in the England team of Basil D'Oliveira, a Cape Coloured player. In 1970, the ICC members voted to suspend South Africa indefinitely from international cricket competition.

Starved of top-level competition for its best players, the South African Cricket Board began funding so-called "rebel tours", offering large sums of money for international players to form teams and tour South Africa. The ICC's response was to blacklist any rebel players who agreed to tour South Africa, banning them from officially sanctioned international cricket. As players were poorly remunerated during the 1970s, several accepted the offer to tour South Africa, particularly players getting towards the end of their careers for which a blacklisting would have little effect.

The rebel tours continued into the 1980s but then progress was made in South African politics and it became clear that apartheid was ending. South Africa, now a "Rainbow Nation" under Nelson Mandela, was welcomed back into international sport in 1991.

- **World Series Cricket**

The money problems of top cricketers were also the root cause of another cricketing crisis that arose in 1977 when the Australian media magnate Kerry Packer fell out with the Australian Cricket Board over TV rights. Taking advantage of the low remuneration paid to players, Packer retaliated by signing several of the best players in the world to a privately run cricket league outside the structure of international cricket. World Series Cricket hired some of the banned South African players and allowed them to show off their skills in an international arena against other world-class players. The schism lasted only until 1979 and the "rebel" players were allowed back into established international cricket, though many found that their national teams had moved on without them. Long-term results of World Series Cricket have included the introduction of significantly higher player salaries and innovations such as coloured kit and night games.

- **Limited-overs cricket**

In the 1960s, English county teams began playing a version of cricket with games of only one innings each and a maximum number of overs per innings. Starting in 1963 as a knockout competition only, limited-overs cricket grew in popularity and, in 1969, a national league was created which consequently caused a reduction in the number of matches in the County Championship. The status of limited overs matches is governed by the official List A categorisation. Although many "traditional" cricket fans objected to the shorter form of the game, limited-overs cricket did have the advantage of delivering a result to spectators within a single day; it did improve cricket's appeal to younger or busier people; and it did prove commercially successful.

The first limited-overs international match took place at Melbourne Cricket Ground in 1971 as a time-filler after a Test match had been abandoned because of heavy rain on the opening days. It was tried simply as an experiment and to give the players some exercise, but turned out to be immensely popular. limited-overs internationals (LOIs or ODIs—one-day internationals) have since grown to become a massively popular form of the game, especially for busy people who want to be able to see a whole match. The International Cricket Council reacted to this development by organising the first Cricket World Cup in England in 1975, with all the Test-playing nations taking part.

- **Analytic and graphic technology**

Limited-overs cricket increased television ratings for cricket coverage. Innovative techniques introduced in coverage of limited-over matches were soon adopted for Test coverage. The innovations included presentation of in-depth statistics and graphical analysis, placing miniature cameras in the stumps, multiple usage of cameras to provide shots from several locations around the ground, high-speed photography and computer graphics technology enabling television viewers to study the course of a delivery and help them understand an umpire's decision.

In 1992, the use of a third umpire to adjudicate run-out appeals with television replays was introduced in the Test series between South Africa and India. The third umpire's duties have subsequently expanded to include decisions on other aspects of play such as stumpings, catches and boundaries. From 2011, the third umpire was being called upon to moderate review of umpires' decisions, including lbw, with the aid of virtual-reality tracking technologies (e.g., Hawk-Eye and Hot Spot), though such measures still could not free some disputed decisions from heated controversy.

- **21st-century cricket**

In June 2001, the ICC introduced a "Test Championship Table" and, in October 2002, a "One-day International Championship Table". As indicated by ICC rankings, the various cricket formats have continued to be a major competitive sport in most former British Empire countries, notably the Indian subcontinent, and new participants including the Netherlands. In 2017, the number of countries with full ICC membership was increased to twelve by the addition of Afghanistan and Ireland.

The ICC expanded its development programme, aiming to produce more national teams capable of competing at the various formats. Development efforts are focused on African and Asian nations, and on the United States. In 2004, the ICC Intercontinental Cup brought first-class cricket to 12 nations, mostly for the first time. Cricket's newest innovation is Twenty20, essentially an evening entertainment. It has so far enjoyed enormous popularity and has attracted large attendances at matches as well as good TV audience ratings. The inaugural ICC Twenty20 World Cup tournament was held in 2007. The formation of Twenty20 leagues in India – the unofficial Indian Cricket League, which started in 2007, and the official Indian Premier League, starting in 2008 – raised much speculation in the cricketing press about their effect on the future of cricket.

FOUR

Gift by the England cricket

- **Gift by the England cricket**

The history of the England cricket team can be said to date back to at least 1739, when sides styled "Kent" and "All England" played a match at Bromley Common. Over 300 matches involving "England" or "All England" prior to 1877 are known. However these teams were usually put together on an ad hoc basis and were rarely fully representative.

The history of the current England side can be traced to 1877 when England played in what was subsequently recognised as the very first Test match. Since then, up to 20 August 2006 they have played 852 Test matches, winning 298, losing 245 and drawing 309. During these 852 matches, they have been captained by 77 different players.

- **Early** history

The term "All-England" was first used in reports of two Kent v All-England matches in July 1739.The first match was at Bromley Common in Kent on Monday 9 July 1739. It was billed as between "eleven gentlemen of that county (i.e., Kent) and eleven gentlemen from any part of England, exclusive of Kent". Kent, described as "the Unconquerable County" won by "a very few notches".

The second match was at the Artillery Ground in Bunhill Fields, Finsbury on Monday 23 July 1739. This game was drawn and a report includes the phrase "eleven picked out of all England".

In subsequent decades there were many more such matches between a side representing a county, or the MCC, and a side drawn from the rest of England and described as "England" or "All England". As the next section describes, in 1846 the term "All England Eleven" would acquire a new, more precise, definition.

- **The All-England XI**

In 1846 William Clarke formed the All-England Eleven as a touring team of leading players to play matches at big city venues, mainly in the North of England. Clarke's team was a top-class side worthy of its title. The AEE lasted until 1880. In 1852, several players set up the United All-England Eleven as a rival to the AEE, and from 1857 to 1866 the annual match between these two teams was arguably the most important contest of the English season – certainly judged by the quality of the players.

- **The 1873/4 team.**

The early overseas tours were organised as purely commercial ventures, as indeed were the first Test-playing tours. The first such tour was to North America by a team of English professionals, departing England in September 1859. The team comprised six players from the All-England Eleven and six from the United All-England Eleven, and was captained by George Parr. They played five matches, winning them all. There were no first-class fixtures.

With the outbreak of the American Civil War, attention turned to Australia. The inaugural tour of the country took place in 1861–2, and was organised by Messrs Spiers & Pond. Led by HH Stephenson, the English team played 12 matches, but none were first-class.

In 1863–4, the Melbourne Cricket Club organised a tour by an English team under the captaincy of George Parr, which also visited New Zealand. The team played 16 matches, but none were first-class.

There were further tours of North America (taking in both the US and Canada) in late 1868, led by Edgar Willsher, and in late 1872, under R.A. Fitzgerald. The latter side included W.G.Grace.

In 1873–4, the Melbourne Cricket Club organised a tour by a team under the captaincy of WG Grace, which played 15 matches, but none were first-class.

Most of the matches of these early touring teams were played "against odds", that is to say the opposing team was permitted to have more than eleven players (usually twenty-two) in order to make a more even contest.

- **1877 to 1890**

James Lillywhite, a professional with Sussex CCC, led a team which had sailed on the P&O steamship Poonah on

21 September 1876. They played in Australia and then New Zealand before returning to Australia to play a combined Australian XI, for once on even terms of XI a side. The match, starting on 15 March 1877 at the Melbourne Cricket Ground, came to be regarded as the first Test match, although none of its participants could have guessed at its significance at the time. Charles Bannerman, of Australia, faced the first ball and scored the first century, a glorious 165 before retiring hurt with a broken finger. The next highest score in this inaugural Test for Australia was Tom Horan with 10. Alfred Shaw of England bowled the first ball and took 5 for 38 in Australia's second innings. Tom Kendall, born in England, took 7 English wickets for 55 to bring Australia victory by 45 runs. 100 years later, in the Centenary Test, the result and margin would be exactly the same. England won a second match to square the series.

In 1878/79 Kent captain and MCC luminary Lord Harris took a team, consisting mainly of amateurs, to Australia where they lost by 10 wickets at Melbourne. Their batting was reasonably strong but the lack of professional bowlers cost them dear. The tour became famous for an unseemly incident in a tour game at Sydney where a near riot broke out. One of the umpires was Edmund Barton, who became Australia's first prime minister.

The 1880 Australian tourists were the first to play a Test match on English soil. Their 'demon' bowler, Fred Spofforth, sustained a hand injury and, crucially, missed the game in which W.G. Grace scored 152 and Billy Murdoch one run better. Lord Harris led the victorious England side at the Oval.

An all professional side, organised by Shaw, Shrewsbury and Lillywhite sailed to Australia for the 1881/82 campaign. The tour was bedeviled with scandal and allegations of fisticuffs, betting and heavy drinking. Tom Garrett took 18 wickets in the three Tests played for Australia. Many of the tour matches were still against local '22's. Australia won the four Test series 2 – 0.

The developing rivalry took on a new turn in 1882, when England lost at home at The Oval in the solitary Test of the summer. Spofforth took 7 for 46 and 7 for 44 and Ted Peate, Yorkshire slow left armer who had taken 8 wickets, was out just 8 runs short of victory. Upset at this turn of events, The Sporting Times printed an obituary to English cricket: "In Affectionate Remembrance of ENGLISH CRICKET, which died at the Oval on 29th AUGUST 1882, Deeply lamented by a large circle of sorrowing friends and acquaintances R.I.P. N.B. – The body will be cremated and the ashes taken to Australia."

When England toured Australia the following winter of 1882/83 and won 2–1, the England captain, the Hon. Ivo Bligh was presented with an urn that contained some ashes, which have variously been said to be of a bail, ball or even a woman's veil. And so The Ashes series was born. Yorkshire stalwart Billy Bates, who played all his 15 Tests on 5 tours to Australia, scored 55 and took 14 for 102 at Melbourne in the second Test, including the first Test hat-trick, to bring England the first innings victory in Test cricket. A.G. Steel made 135* at Sydney – although he did drop Bonner 4 times (out of 8 drops in total) as the giant Australian hitter scored 87.

England won 1–0 in the three Test series in 1884. Peate took 6 for 85 in Australia's first innings, and Ulyett 7 for 36, the second as England won by an innings Lord's where Steel made a wonderful 148 out of England's first innings of 379. Australia's captain Billy Murdoch scored the first Test double hundred at the Oval where Walter Read of England hit a century in 113 minutes after going in at number 10. All 11 Englishmen bowled in Australia's innings, including wicket keeper Lyttelton with underarm lobs.

England embarked on a long stretch of dominance. They won 14 and lost only 3 of the Tests played between 1884 and 1890. Billy Barnes hit 134 in the opening Adelaide Test of the five Test 1884/85 series while Johnny Briggs of Lancashire hit a two-hour ton at Melbourne in the second, where Australia fielded a completely new team of 11 different players after a dispute over gate money. Wilfred Flowers scored 56 and took 5 for 46 in the third Test at Sydney where Australia pulled back a game thanks to Bonner smashing a century in even time. England won the deciding fifth Test by an innings at Melbourne, Arthur Shrewsbury making 105*.

W. G. Grace scored 170 in the Oval Test of 1886, beating the individual Test innings record of 164 set by Arthur Shrewsbury in the previous match on an evil pitch at Lords. England won by an innings on the third day after Australia were bowled out for 68 and 149m with George Lohmann of Surrey taking 12 for 104. The Australian tourists, without Bannerman or Murdoch and often losing Spofforth to injuries, lost all three Tests.

Shrewsbury's England beat Australia in both matches on the 1886–87 tour, despite being bowled out for 45 on the first day at Sydney. Two England parties toured there in 1887–88, with Shaw and Shrewsbury's team sponsored by Melbourne CC and Lord Harris's team by the Sydney Association. The two sides joined up for one Test Match at Sydney which they won thanks to Lohmann's 9 wickets and Bobby Peel's 10. Australia made just 42 and 82 on a poor pitch in bad light.

The 1888 Australians won at Lords but lost at The Oval and Old Trafford. Their bowling was penetrative, particularly Jack Ferris and the 'terror' Charlie Turner, but their batting was too weak to withstand the English professionals in their home conditions. Bobby Peel took 11 wickets at Old Trafford.

England won the first Test in South Africa, at Port Elizabeth in March 1889 by 8 wickets, despite fielding a less than first choice XI. W.H. Ashley took 7 for 95 for South Africa in his only Test. Bobby Abel of Surrey scored 120 for England in the Second Test, the first hundred scored in South Africa. Bernard Tancred of South Africa became the first Test batsman to carry his bat, for 26*, as South Africa collapsed to 47 all out. M.P. Bowden remains the youngest man to captain England, at just 23 years and 144 days. Johnny Briggs took 7 for 17 and 8 for 11 at Cape Town, 14 bowled and 1 LBW.

- **1890s**

Four ball overs gave way to five ball overs in the 1890s and to six ball overs in Australia, as the game continued to develop quickly. England won the 1890 Ashes series 2–0, although Jack Barrett carried his bat for 67 through Australia's second innings of 176 at Lord's. W. G. Grace was out second ball in the first innings but saw England home in the second with 75*. Frederick Martin took 12 Australian wickets for 102 but 'Nutty' never played an Ashes match again. The third scheduled match, at Old Trafford, was the first Test to be abandoned without a ball being bowled.

W. G. Grace's tourists lost 2–1 on the 1891–92 tour, Australia winning at Melbourne and Sydney, where Bannerman batted for seven and a half hours and scored only three boundaries and England's Bobby Abel carried his bat for 132. England claimed a consolation innings victory at Adelaide where Stoddard scored 134 and Peel 83 and Briggs took 6 wickets in each innings.

England won the only Test on the 1891/92 tour of South Africa at Cape Town, where Harry Wood, the Surrey wicket keeper made 134 not out and Ferris, who had earlier played for Australia, took 13 for 91. Billy Murdoch was another Australian turned Englishman on the tour.

- England regained the Ashes in 1893, with an innings win at The Oval and draws in the other two Tests. W. G. Grace and A.E. Stoddart made three consecutive century opening stands. William Gunn of Nottinghamshire scored his only Test hundred, 102*, at Old Trafford, while Arthur Shrewsbury scored 106 at Lord's. Future England great Ranjitsinhji was one of the unfortunate bowlers as Australia set a new record team score of 843 against 'Oxford and Cambridge Past and Present' in Portsmouth.

Andrew Stoddart led England to a thrilling 3–2 victory on the 1894–1895 Ashes tour. Bobby Peel took the final wickets in the first Test victory at Sydney and the second at Melbourne and hit the winning runs in the final and deciding Test at the MCG. England's amazing victory at Sydney, by 10 runs, came after they had followed on with Lancashire's Albert Ward hitting 75 and 117 in the game. J.T. Brown scored 140 for England at Melbourne where England were set 297 to win. He reached 50 in 28 minutes and put on a then record 210 with Ward as England won by six wickets. Tom Richardson took 32 wickets in the Tests.

- England won all three Tests of the 1895/96 tour of South Africa by resounding margins. Lohmann was unplayable, taking 7 for 38 and 8 for 7 at Port Elizabeth and finishing with a hat trick. He took 9 for 28 and 3 for 43 at Johannesburg and 7 for 42 and 1 for 45 at Cape Town.

Having been overlooked for the first Test at Lord's, where Australian captain Harry Trott scored 143 and put on a record 210 with Syd Gregory (103), Shri Ranjitsinhji burst into Test cricket with 62 and 154 at Old Trafford in 1896. His magical batting and Tom Richardson's 13 for 244 were not enough to prevent Australia running out winners by 3 wickets however. Five English professionals went on 'strike' for more money before the Oval Test. Abel, Hayward and Richardson relented, but Gunn and Lohmann never played for England again. England won the series 2–1.

The Ashes were lost on Andrew Stoddart's 1897/98 tour, with Australia thumping England 4–1. Australian Joe Darling was the first batsmen to make 500 runs in a Test series, including 101 at Sydney, 178 at Adelaide and 160 in the final Sydney Test, where his hundred came up in 91 minutes. Stoddart's mother died just before the first Test and he was too distraught to play in either of the first two matches. Ranji, batting at number 7 after a throat infection, scored a brilliant 175 in the first Test and took England over 500 for the first time in a game won by 9 wickets but the Englishmen lost the next four heavily.

Lord Hawke's tourists in 1898/99 played and won two Tests in South Africa, with sometime Australian Albert Trott taking 17 wickets. Plum Warner carried his bat for 132 at Johannesburg in his maiden Test.

The 1899 series against Australia saw two significant developments. For the first time in England, five Tests were played rather than three, with Trent Bridge and Headingley being added to the "traditional" venues of Lord's, The Oval and Old Trafford. Also MCC and the counties appointed a selection committee for the first time. It comprised three active players: Lord Hawke, W.G. Grace and H.W. Bainbridge who was the captain of Warwickshire. Prior to this, England teams for home Tests had been chosen by the club on whose ground the match was to be played. The peerless Australian Victor Trumper dominated the series. He scored 1,500 runs on the tour, including 300 not out against Sussex and a breathtaking century in Australia's sole, but deciding, Test victory at Lords. W.G. Grace played his last Test at Trent Bridge. F.S. Jackson and Tom Hayward put on 185 at the Oval for the first wicket. England, scoring 576, forced Australia (352) to follow on, but the Australians played out the draw and with it retained the Ashes.

- **1900–1914: The "Golden Age"**

The first Test series of the new century took place in Australia 1901–1902 and was won by Australia who came from one down to take the series 4–1. The England side was a private venture of Archie MacLaren (although the matches were all official Test matches). It was rather an attritional series of matches with only three centuries being scored and only one team innings over 400 (the first innings of England in the First Test at the SCG). Sydney Barnes made his debut for England and took 19 wickets in the first two Tests before being injured in the third and talking no further part in the series.

There was a home series against Australia in 1902 which was won by the Australians (2–1). In the drawn First Test at Edgbaston Australia were dismissed for 36 in their first innings (Wilfred Rhodes 7 for 17) but rain meant that the match was drawn. Rain also ruined the following match at

Lord's. Sydney Barnes returned to the England team and had immediate success, taking seven wickets in the third Test at Sheffield (the only Test ever to be played there).

However England still lost the match. The final two Tests were amongst the most exciting of all time. A brilliant century by Trumper helped Australia to win the match at Old Trafford by three runs. England's batting throughout the series was modest with only one innings of over 300 and with only three centuries scored. The last of these was a match-winning innings in the final Test at The Oval by Gilbert Jessop, who went in at number seven in the second innings with England 48–5 and scored what was then the fastest century in Test cricket in 70 minutes, setting up an improbable England win by one wicket. The last wicket pair of Wilfred Rhodes and George Hirst nervelessly acquired the final fifteen runs needed for victory.

England toured Australia in 1903–1904, the first time that the MCC had been responsible for an England tour overseas. England regained The Ashes with a 3–2 series win under the captaincy of Plum Warner. In the first Test R.E.Foster made his Test debut and scored 287 in his first ever innings – the then highest ever Test score and a record that was to stand for a quarter of a century. Wilfred Rhodes took 15 wickets in England's second Test win at the MCG –a record that was to stand for thirty years. In the fifth Test England were dismissed for 61 in their first innings on a rain-affected pitch.

In 1905 Australia toured England and were beaten 2–0 with three matches drawn. Notable batting performances in the series included centuries by A.C. MacLaren, F.S. Jackson (2), Johnny Tyldesley (2) and C.B. Fry. B.J.T. Bosanquet, the inventor of the googly, took eight wickets in an Innings in the First Test.

In 1905–06 Plum Warner took an MCC team to South Africa for the first time and England were soundly beaten 4–1 in the series. England's batting faltered throughout the series with only one team innings in excess of 200 (successive innings of 184,190,148,160,295,196,198,160,187 and 130) and just one individual century (by F.L.Fane in the 3rd Test at the Wanderers). England's only win came at Newlands where the left-arm slow bowler Colin Blythe took eleven wickets in the match.

In 1907 there was a home three match Test series against South Africa which England, captained by R.E.Foster, won 1–0. Highlights included another sparkling innings by Gilbert Jessop who scored 93 at Lord's in a partnership of 145 for the sixth wicket with Len Braund who scored a century. There was another fine bowling performance by Blythe, who took 15 wickets at Headingley on a rain-affected match in a match that England won despite having been bowled out for 76 in their first innings.

In England's Test series in Australia in 1907–08 Australia won the first Test but England hit back well with a narrow win at the MCG in the 2nd Test in which Jack Hobbs made his England debut scoring 83 and 28. England were outplayed by Australia in the next three Tests and lost the series and the Ashes 4–1. England's batting was fragile throughout the series with only Gunn (2) and Hutchings scoring hundreds. The bowling relied on Jack Crawford), Arthur Fielder and Barnes, who took 79 wickets between them.

In a home series against Australia in 1909 England lost 2–1 (two draws) and no combination of players (England used 25 in total in the series) seemed to work. England failed to make 200 in an innings five times and there was only one individual century (by J. Sharp in the 3rd Test). The remarkable Colin Blythe delivered England's only victory by taking eleven wickets in the First Test at Edgbaston, but thereafter Australia, whilst never dominating the England attack, always had the edge.

England returned to South Africa in 1909–10 under H.D.G. Leveson-Gower, for a five match Test series and fared little better than on their first visit in 1905–06. The series was lost 3–2 but this disguises South Africa's superiority. The main highlight was Jack Hobbs first (of 15) Test century in the final Test at Newlands, he put on a then record 211 for the first wicket with Wilfred Rhodes. This was one of only two personal hundreds by England batsmen in the series. The bowling attack was weak – although the last of the great "lob" (underhand) bowlers George Simpson-Hayward had field days in the first three Test matches when he took a total of 21 wickets. Colin Blythe bowled England to a consolation win in the fifth Test with ten wickets in the match. Legspin dominated on the matting pitches, with the ball often bouncing chest high. Vogler took 29 wickets for the home side and Faulkner 29.

England toured Australia in 1911/12 under Plum Warner, but Johnny Douglas took over the captaincy when Warner fell ill prior to the first Test. Despite losing that first match at Sydney, a side which boasted Jack Hobbs, Frank Woolley, Sydney Barnes and Wilfred Rhodes hit back to take the next four Tests in style. Frank Foster and Barnes dominated with the ball, sharing 66 wickets, while Hobbs, Rhodes and Woolley recorded centuries. Hobbs and Rhodes shared opening stands of 147 at Adelaide and a then record 323 at Melbourne in the next Test where Barnes dismissed Bardsley, Kelleway, Hill and Armstrong for 3 runs in his opening spell. Later in the game, when the crowd barracked Barnes for deliberating over a field setting, he threw the ball down in disgust and refused to continue until order was restored. Frank Woolley also hit 305* in 205 minutes in a tour game against Tasmania.

The 1912 home season saw a unique experiment with a 9 Test triangular tournament involving South Africa and Australia but it was an idea ahead of its time and was not repeated. C.B. Fry of Sussex captained the team against Syd Gregory of Australia and Frank Mitchell of South Africa. Jack Hobbs scored 107 against Australia at Lords in a rain ruined game. The Australia v South Africa match, at Lord's, was notable for a visit by King George V, the first time a reigning monarch had watched Test cricket. Barnes took 34 wickets in his 3 Tests against the South Africans.

England's 1913/14 tour of South Africa was the last before the onset of World War I, and England dominated the rubber, winning 4–0. Syd Barnes was once again unplayable, taking 49 wickets in four Tests before boycotting the last in a row over his wife's accommodation. Only Herbie Taylor resisted for the home side, with skilful backfoot defence on the matting pitches, scoring 508 runs at 50.8.

- **1920s**

England resumed their Test cricket after World War I with a tour of Australia in 1920/21 under Johnny Douglas. After the ravages of the war it was little surprise when England went down to a series of crushing defeats, the first 5–0 whitewash. Six Australians scored hundreds while Mailey spun out 36 English batsmen. Things were no better when Warwick Armstrong's men toured England in 1921. Australian fast bowlers Gregory and McDonald battered the English batsmen with a succession of bouncers and Jack Hobbs missed most of the season with first a leg injury then appendicitis. England used 30 players in all. Only one Australian made a century as opposed to 3 for England – A. C. "Jack" Russell scoring 101 and 102* and Phil Mead 182* – but Australia's 3–0 victory made it 8 Ashes defeats in succession.

England resumed the winning habit on the 1922/23 tour of South Africa, under F.T. Mann, winning a pulsating rubber 2 – 1. England lost the first Test but scraped to victory in the next, at Cape Town, by one wicket. Phil Mead scored 181 at Kingsmead, Durban, to ensure a draw and they won the fifth and final match, also at Durban, thanks to Jack Russell's twin centuries in his final Test. This dominance was underlined in England in 1924 with a 3–0 for England.

Hopes that the Ashes might be regained were dashed on the 1924/25 tour down under however, Australia thrashing England 4–1, although England scored 8 centuries to Australia's 6. Herbert Sutcliffe scored 734 runs at 81.56 and Maurice Tate broke Mailey's Ashes record with 38 wickets, bowling 2,528 balls in the Tests. England's only victory came at Melbourne, by an innings, after Captain Arthur Gilligan won the toss for the only time. It was England's first Ashes Test win in 12 years.

England drew the first four Tests of the 1926 Ashes series and so the series rested on the Oval Test, for which Percy Chapman replaced Arthur Carr as captain and both the 48-year-old Rhodes and 21-year-old Larwood were selected. Hobbs and Sutcliffe scored centuries and Australia lost by 289 runs. The South African team proved stronger than before however and drew the 1927/28 series 2–2.

A fourth team was, at last, introduced to Test cricket when the West Indies took their bow in 1928. England won each of the three Tests by an innings, Freeman taking 22 wickets, and a view was expressed in the press that their elevation had proved a mistake although 'electric heels' Learie Constantine did the double on the tour. The England team at this period was as strong as it has ever been and Australia were dispatched 4–1 on the 1928/29 Ashes tour. Hammond scored 44, 28, 251, 200, 32, 119*, 177, 38 and 16 – a total of 905 runs, a new record. Percy Chapman captained the team but barely played again.

England, under J. C. White and Arthur Carr, beat South Africa 2–0 at home in 1929 with Herbert Sutcliffe scoring a hundred in each innings at the Oval Bizarrely there were two concurrent England tours in 1929/30, one to New Zealand and one to the West Indies. Surrey paceman Maurice Allom took four wickets in five balls in New Zealand's maiden Test match, including a hat trick, and his 8 for 65 swept England to victory in Christchurch by 8 wickets with the three later Tests drawn. At the same time another England team were drawing 1–1 in the West Indies under F. S. G. Calthorpe. Forty-year-old Patsy Hendren made 1,765 runs on this tour and Andy Sandham scored 325 at Kingston (out of England's 849) in his final Test. The 'black Bradman' George Headley followed twin centuries at Georgetown with 223 in the same Kingston game.

- **1930s**

The 21-year-old Don Bradman dominated the 1930 Ashes series in England, scoring 974 runs in his seven Test innings. He scored 254 at Lord's, 334 at Headingley, when Chapman stuck to attacking fields all day, and 232 at the Oval. Australia regained the Ashes. Harold Larwood took only four wickets in the series although K. S. Duleepsinhji made 173 at Lord's on debut.

England played five Tests in South Africa on the 1930/31 tour. Chasing 240 to win the first Test at the Old Wanderers ground in Johannesburg they were bowled out by E. P. Nupen, a master on the matting wicket, and drew the next four.

New Zealand played their first Test in England in 1931 and their strong performance at Lord's led the authorities to arrange another two that summer, one of which England won. India played their first Test in England in 1932 at Lords, reducing England to 19 for 3 on the first morning before losing a competitive match when they were bowled out for 187 chasing 346.

Bill Woodfull evades a Bodyline ball. Note the number of leg-side fielders.

Before the 1932–3 tour to Australia, England had become used to the prolific run-scoring of Don Bradman. The England captain, Surrey's Douglas Jardine chose to develop the already existing leg theory into fast leg theory, or bodyline, as a tactic to stop Bradman. Fast leg theory involved bowling fast balls directly at the batsman's body, and Jardine had two very fast accurate bowlers, Harold Larwood and Bill Voce to bowl them. The batsman would need to defend himself, and if he touched the ball with the bat, he risked being caught by one of a large number of fielders placed on the leg side.

England won the series and the Ashes 4–1. But complaints about the Bodyline tactic caused crowd disruption on the tour, and threats of diplomatic action from the Australian Cricket Board, which during the tour sent the following cable to the Marylebone Cricket Club in London:

Bodyline bowling assumed such proportions as to menace best interests of game, making protection of body by batsmen the main consideration. Causing intensely bitter feeling between players as well as injury. In our opinion is unsportsmanlike. Unless stopped at once likely to upset friendly relations existing between Australia and England.

Later, Jardine was removed from the captaincy and the laws of cricket changed so that no more than one fast ball aimed at the body was permitted per over, and having more than two fielders behind square leg were banned.

England won two Tests on the 1933/34 tour of India, the first ever Tests held in the sub continent. England won by nine wickets at Bombay's Gymkhana ground with Bryan Valentine scoring 136 in his first Test innings. Morris Nichols and E. W. "Nobby" Clark bowled so many bouncers at the Indian batsman that they wore solar topees instead of caps to protect themselves from the ball as much as the sun. Naoomal Jeoomal top edged a Clark bouncer into his head in the third Test, was unable to continue and didn't bat in the second innings.

Australia won the first Test of the 1934 Ashes series by 238 runs at Trent Bridge. Clarrie Grimmett took 25 wickets in the series, and Bill O'Reilly 28 as England were spun to defeat. Bradman made 758 runs in the Tests and 2020 on the tour, with Stan McCabe making 2078. Patsy Hendren(132) and Maurice Leyland (153) ensured a draw at Old Trafford and England did manage a rare Test win over Australia at Lord's with Hedley Verity taking 14 wickets in a day and 15 in the match. Bradman (304) and Ponsford (181) put on 388 at Headingley and then 451 at the Oval where England lost by a massive 562 runs. Ponsford scored 266 in his last Test. Nobby Clark bowled some 'leg theory' against the Australians, with little success. Bill Voce took 8 for 66 for Notts against the Australians but withdrew from the attack with a 'leg injury' after Woodfall raised discrete objections.

England toured the West Indies in 1934/5 and showed the folly of sending a weakened team as they lost the rubber 2–1 with George Headley scoring 270 not out in the 4th Test at Sabina Park. South Africa won on English soil for the first time, taking the 5 Test series 1–0 in 1935 with a victory at Lord's by 157 runs thanks to Bruce Mitchell's 164 and Jock Cameron's quickfire 90. Cameron died at 30, of enteric fever, soon after returning home from this tour.

India used 22 players in three Tests in England in 1936. A then record 588 runs were scored on the second day of the Old Trafford Test and England too experimented with their team and took the rubber 2–0.

The 1936/37 Ashes tour, under Gubby Allen, was a titanic struggle. England, helped by rain freshening the pitch, won by 322 runs in Brisbane and an innings in Sydney where Wally Hammond scored 271 not out. Bill Voce was their spearhead, taking 17 wickets in these two games. Bradman added a record 346 for the sixth wicket with Jack Fingleton at Melbourne and followed that with 212 at Adelaide where his team leveled the score at 2–2. Bradman, McCabe and Badcock all scored hundreds in the decider at Melbourne and Australian took the series 3–2.

England beat New Zealand 1–0 in a three Test rubber in 1937. Tom Goddard took 6 for 29 in bowling out the visitors for 134 at the Old Trafford Test as they chased 265 to win. Jack Cowie had taken 6 for 67 for New Zealand and 10 in the match. Len Hutton scored a century after having begun his England career with 0 and 1 at Lords. Prospective tours of South Africa and West Indies fell through in the winter of 1937/38.

The 1938 Ashes series was a high scoring affair. Hutton, Barnett, Paynter (216*) and Compton made hundreds at

Trent Bridge with the Australians scoring three including Stan McCabe's brilliant 232.

Hammond scored 240 in the Lord's Test while Bill Brown made a double ton and Bradman a match saving century for Australia. Old Trafford fell victim to the rain and Australia retained the Ashes with a win at Headingley, thanks to Bradman's century and 10 wickets for O'Reilly and 7 for Fleetwood-Smith. England won the final Test at the Oval thanks to a record Test score of 903 – 7 dec and Len Hutton's world record of 364 in 13 hours, 17 minutes. Bradman, whose score of 334 had been surpassed, was the first to congratulate the 22-year-old Yorkshireman. Maurice Leyland made 187 and the elegant Joe Hardstaff 169 not out. Australia subsided to 201 and 123, batting 2 short, and England won by an innings and 579.

Paul Gibb scored 93 and 106 on debut at Johannesburg on England's 1938/39 tour. England scored 11 centuries in the series and South Africa 6. Paynter scored 117 and 100 in the first Test and 243 in the third at Durban. England, 1–0, in the series, returned to Durban to play a deciding 'timeless' Test to the finish. It was abandoned as a draw after 10 days as England had to catch the train to catch the boat home. Needing 696 to win they were, incredibly, 654 for 5, Gibb having scored 120, Hammond 140 and Edrich 219. A record 1981 runs were scored, and the concept of timeless Tests was abandoned.

The three Tests between England and the West Indies in 1939 were the last before the Second World War, although a team for an MCC tour of India was selected more in hope than expectation of the matches being played. Len Hutton and Denis Compton, leaders of the bright new batting generation, scored hundreds at Lords where the brilliant George Headley scored a ton in each innings. Hammond became the first fielder to hold 100 Test catches at Old Trafford. England took the series 1–0 as the war clouds loomed over Europe.

Printed by Libri Plureos GmbH in Hamburg,
Germany